M000073066

A Birthday Astrologer

0 43422 69524 9

Copyright © 1998 , Great Quotations Publishing Co.

Illustrations by S.Papel & Co.

Page Design & Typesetting by Bostrom Publishing, Inc.

This book is intended for use as entertainment only
and does not reflect in any way the religious views of this company.

Printed in Hong Kong

TO:

FROM:

DATE:

Introduction

"Thou canst not stir a flower
Without troubling of a star."
--Francis Thompson (English poet)

Astrology is a complex science. This is a simple book.

We will scratch the surface of the ancient wisdom of the stars, developed 6,000 years ago.
We're not going to get technical. We're going to have a little fun.

We're going to help you choose a gift for snooty Taurus (polyester offends them) and plan a party
for suspicious Scorpio. (Throw a surprise party, and he's likely to storm out the door–if you're lucky.)
We're going to list each sign's flowers, gemstone and colors, track the prospects for
astrological match-ups. And, as an added bonus, we're offering a hip, '90s listing of who was born
in your sign and on *your* birthday. We're talking Madonna and Bill Clinton (both Leos)
–not a bunch of silent movie stars you've never heard of.

We're going to help you understand your friends and enemies a little better
–and avoid birthday disasters.

Table of Contents

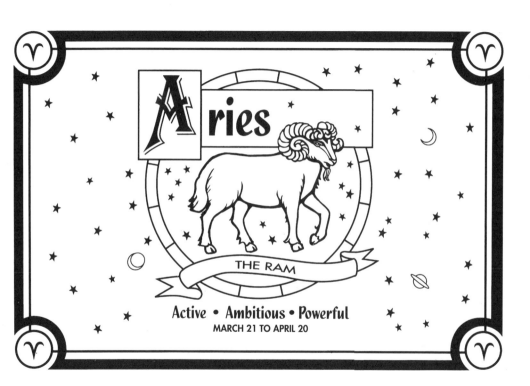

Active • Ambitious • Powerful
MARCH 21 TO APRIL 20

1

The Aries Personality: "Me First"

Go ahead. Tell a Ram to follow the leader. Then stand back (or run). He'll stomp around, fume, flail his arms angrily. Rams don't follow. They lead.
Everyone should know that.

Rams know what they want, and they always get it. If they don't get it *now*, they throw temper tantrums. Like spoiled children.

Scarlett O'Hara was an Aries. Get the picture?

Driven? Rams put Hurricane Andrew to shame.
Aries are commandos. They're ruled by Mars,
the fiery red planet that inspired the God of War.
They think the Huns were wimps.

Spend a day with an Aries. You'll need a week in bed
to recover. They whirl around and around like the
Tazmanian Devil. It's exhausting just to *watch* them.
Don't try to keep up. It's not possible.

You never have to question where a Ram stands—
on *anything*. Rams tell you everything you want
to know, and then some, about themselves.
"But we've talked about me long enough," they'll say.
"What do *you* think about me?"

You think they don't notice, or care, if you're listening.
But deep inside, they're really afraid you won't like them.
They need to be loved—by everybody.

The Aries Friend

Rams know everyone—and make lots of noise so everyone knows them. They want to be everybody's friend. They're not picky. They like anyone who will listen to *them*.

Rams want their friends to be successful and spectacular, to make *them* look good.

They're not afraid to ask for favors—big ones. They'll do the same for you—if they're around. An Aries may drop out of your life for months, even years, then drop back in when you least expect it.

The Aries Lover

Rams *expect* to be swept off their feet with searing,
red-hot, heart-in-your-mouth, bells-and-whistles passion.
They're in love with falling madly in love. (They don't
necessarily love the object of their affections–
it's the excitement of the fall that gets them.)

They're amorous. Better keep up, or they'll satisfy their urges
elsewhere. When the thrill is gone, so are they.

They ain't easy to live with. They marry late or not at all.
They often divorce. They believe in themselves
far more than anybody else.

An Astrological Compatibility Guide

Aries and Aries: Spontaneous combustion. The fireworks are
spectacular and scary. They butt heads but resolve their
fierce arguments with hot, sweaty lovemaking. Steamy.

Aries and Taurus: Forgetaboutit. Rams act without thinking,
speak without thinking, and ram anything in their way.
Stubborn, practical Bulls are in their way.

Aries and Gemini: Like two kids in Candyland, they skip off
hand in hand, convinced they can rule the world.
A beautiful fantasy for them. Scary for the rest of the world.
Anything can happen.

Aries and Cancer: Rams attack; Crabs retreat. The two have different ideas about everything from the meaning of life to buttering toast. A painful match.

Aries and Leo: Rams and Lions coo over each other and get hot flashes when they're together. Even their fierce clashes of strong wills are exciting.

Aries and Virgo: Rams are fiery, flighty and despise practical people. Virgos are practical people. Bad idea.

Aries and Libra: Gentle Libra is among the few who can soften the excitable Ram. Libra respects the Ram's *cahones.* Opposites can attract. But it takes a lot of work.

Aries and Scorpio: Danger. Rams demand to be the aggressor. Scorpions demand to be the aggressor. Scorpions love secrets. Rams can't keep them. Stand clear.

Aries and Sagittarius: They both believe in Santa Claus, telling the truth even if it hurts, and talking. And talking. And talking. If they can shut up long enough to listen to each other, this match is made in heaven.

Aries and Capricorn: The Ram lives by his wits. The Goat plans out which socks he will wear the night before. Where Capricorn finds peace, Aries finds boredom. Only the sure-footed would attempt this rocky climb.

Aries and Aquarius: Fascinating. Together, they will fight for justice in Khartoum, study Buddhism in Tibet. A powerful union, but the Aquarian's natural interest in (gasp) *others* will miff self-centered Aries.

Aries and Pisces: The Ram will trample all over watery, supersensitive Pisces. The Fish lives in a fantasy world all his own; the Ram knows only reality. A masochistic match, once you get past the sexual chemistry.

Happy Birthday, Aries

Rams love gifts—the more expensive, the better. They *require* diamonds. If you can't afford a few carats, glass (crystal, of course) will do.

Personalize the gift with the Ram's name or monogram. They eat that up. They need to know it has been specially chosen *just* for them—that it's not some remnant you picked up on the sale table at Walmart.

Wrap it obnoxiously. Make it as ostentatious as you can bear. Shiny wrapping paper turns them on.

Flowers: Thistles, honeysuckle, and daisies.

Jewels: Diamond (what else?). In ancient times, only kings could own the brilliant stones. The name diamond means "invincible."

Clothing: Aries like bright, dramatic, attention-getting attire.

Colors: Red, gold and deep blue.

Food: Aries like onions, leeks, hops (the stuff in beer)–strong-tasting foods for strong-tasting people.

Throw A Party: Any party fit for an Aries will be obnoxiously huge (rent a convention center–or at least a beer hall). Invite every single person they know–and bring in a few extras. Sing "Happy Birthday" at least two dozen times. Hang red banners with their names on them. Act as if their birthday is a national holiday. *They* think it should be.

Birthday Directory

(Other Rams of Fame and Fortune)

March 21: Eric Rohmer
Johann Sebastian Bach

March 22: Andrew Lloyd Webber
Pat Robertson

March 23: Joan Crawford
Amanda Plummer

March 24: Harry Houdini
Steve McQueen

March 25: Anita Bryant
Aretha Franklin

March 26: Robert Frost
Erica Jong

March 27: Sarah Vaughan
Michael York

March 28: Edmund Muskie
Reba McEntire

March 29: John McLaughlin
Kurt Thomas

March 30: Warren Beatty
Eric Clapton

March 31: Rhea Perlman
Herb Alpert

April 1: Jane Powell
Debbie Reynolds

April 2: Hans Christian Anderson
Jack Webb

April 3: Marlon Brando
Eddie Murphy

April 4: Muddy Waters
John Cameron Swayze

April 5: Bette Davis
Gregory Peck

April 6: Merle Haggard
Billy Dee Williams

April 7: David Frost
Billie Holiday

April 8: Mary Pickford
John Schneider

April 9: Keshia Knight Pulliam
Dennis Quaid

April 10: Joseph Pulitzer
Harry Morgan

April 11: Ethel Kennedy
Leo Rosten

April 12: David Letterman
Tiny Tim

April 13: Lyle Waggoner
Ricky Schroeder

April 14: Julie Christie
Anthony Perkins

April 15: Henry James
Bessie Smith

April 16: Charlie Chaplin
Wilbur Wright

April 17: William Holden
Nikita Khrushchev

April 18: James Woods
Eric Roberts

April 19: Dudley Moore
Eliot Ness

April 20: Joan Miro
Ryan O'Neal

Taurus

THE BULL

Possessive • Enterprising • Determined
APRIL 21 TO MAY 22

The Taurus Personality: "Count On Me"

Strong. Steady. Reliable. Decisive. Bulls ain't glamorous. You might even call them boring (and they won't be all that offended). They ooze common sense. They always finish what they start. They always do what they promise.

Taurus is the sign you turn to when your car breaks down, your finances are in ruins, or your wife has left you. They have strong shoulders and good advice.

15

Bulls plod through life building a solid career, a quality home and a healthy family. They hoard their pennies and fill their houses with fine things. A plush velvet sofa makes Taurus feel all warm inside.

Bulls are earth mothers (and fathers). Their one weakness is indulgence–they can never get enough food, relaxation, or sex (preferably all at the same time).

Bulls are charming in a slow, sensual kind of way.
They're funny. They don't mind poking fun
at themselves to make you laugh.

Don't let that fool you. Bulls are stubborn. New ideas
make them nervous, and they don't like to be pushed.
It takes a lot to make them *mad,* but then they get mad.
They won't forget their grudge for a long time
(and neither will you).

The Taurus Friend

Tauruses don't trust just anyone. Tell them your deepest secrets within minutes of meeting them, and watch them run. Bulls make friends slowly and cautiously (like they do everything else). They keep a circle of close, intimate pals.

You want to be in that circle. Bulls are friends for life. They keep secrets. They're not afraid to tell you when you're being stupid. They invite you to their luxurious homes and lavish you with fine food and wine. They'll do almost anything (that's legal) to make you happy.

18

The Taurus Lover

Bulls need cows to protect and love. They're the marrying kind. They start sizing up your possibilities moments after they meet you. They woo you with quiet, candlelit evenings in their romantic love nests. They get you between their fine linen sheets. They are highly sexual animals.

Tauruses are never afraid to say "I love you." They're snuggly and cuddly. Sometimes they give too much and forget to take back. All they ask is that you never, *ever* cheat on them. Bulls are fiercely possessive. When betrayed, they're merciless. They paw the ground, snort—and *charge*.

An Astrological Compatibility Guide

Taurus and Aries: Forgetaboutit. Rams act without thinking, speak without thinking, and ram anything in their way. Stubborn, practical Bulls are in their way.

Taurus and Taurus: Stability squared. A match as comfortable (and just as exciting) as a cozy old sweater. They'll spend half their lives in the kitchen, the other half in the bedroom. So, they're in a rut. Who cares?

Taurus and Gemini: Routine gives Gemini the jitters. Routine gives Taurus hot flashes. The only thing the Bull can rely on is the Twins' unreliability. A rotten idea.

Taurus and Cancer: These two have the rare ability to be soul mates, business partners and lovers—all at once. A union even Bogey and Bacall would envy.

Taurus and Leo: Overbearing Leo will set the Bull to stomping his feet and tossing his horns. Leo needs the freedom of the jungle; Bulls need to keep an eye on their cows. An incompatible combination.

Taurus and Virgo: Both are practical, earthy, principled. A sensible, stable union likely to result in a house in the suburbs and 2.5 kids.

Taurus and Libra: Libra's flirting will drive Taurus crazy. Libra yawns at the Bull's routines. Both signs appreciate the arts. Limit the relationship to monthly trips to the museum.

Taurus and Scorpio: The most divine enemies in the Zodiac. They admire and envy each other, but would rather die than admit it. Run, don't walk, from this fatal attraction.

Taurus with Sagittarius: Sagittarius lives for adventure; Taurus lives for cozy nights by the fire. Sagittarius can't sit still; Taurus is a lounging pro. A mismatch.

Taurus and Capricorn: Carefully planned destiny. Their solid love results in a church wedding, well-mannered children, and a fat pension fund. Dan Quayle, eat your heart out. We're talking family values here.

Taurus and Aquarius: Aquarius moves a step ahead; Taurus plods slowly with the crowd. Aquarians need detachment; Bulls need devotion. Their differences are so huge they need a translator to say hello.

Taurus and Pisces: Pisces is a fantasy addict; Taurus a harsh realist. The dreamy Fish's illusions will drive the earthy Bull to murder. A masochistic match-up.

23

Happy Birthday, Taurus

Shopping for a Taurus? Bring lots of cash.

Bulls are snobs. They like fine, well-made (translation: *expensive*) things. Polyester offends them. It's better to buy them a key chain handcrafted in Italy than an entire suitcase made in Taiwan. *Quality,* not quantity.

Make it easy on yourself. Just give them the cash. No one loves money like the Bull. If you must shop for a Taurus, don't expect lavish thanks. Bulls are better at receiving than giving.

Flowers: Daisies, pink roses, poppies, and violets.

Jewels: Emerald. It is reputed to bring good memory, happy families and safe journeys.

Clothing: Bulls like tailored, conservative clothes of the highest quality cut and fabric.

Colors: Pale blue, pink, green, and pastels.

Food: Tauruses *love* food. Wheat and cereals, berries, apples, pears, grapes, artichokes and beans are associated with them. They'd rather have something chocolate or decadent.

Throw A Party: An intimate, extravagant dinner party for a handful of close friends would be best for the stay-at-home Bull. The wine should be first-class, the gourmet meal served in twelve courses, and the cake, rich flourless chocolate fudge.

Birthday Directory

(Other Bulls of Fame and Fortune)

April 21:	Queen Elizabeth II Tony Danza	
April 22:	Peter Frampton Jack Nicholson	
April 23:	Valerie Bertinelli William Shakespeare	
April 24:	Barbra Streisand Richard Daley	
April 25:	Al Pacino Ella Fitzgerald	
April 26:	Carol Burnett Bobby Rydell	
April 27:	Sheena Easton Ulysses S. Grant	
April 28:	James Baker III Jay Leno	
April 29:	Michelle Pfeiffer Duke Ellington	
April 30:	Willie Nelson Isiah Thomas	
May 1:	Judy Collins Rita Coolidge	

May 2:	Bing Cosby Saddam Hussein
May 3:	Christopher Cross James Brown
May 4:	Audrey Hepburn Randy Travis
May 5:	Karl Marx Sigmund Freud
May 6:	Willie Mays Bob Seger
May 7:	Willard Scott Janis Ian
May 8:	Melissa Gilbert Harry S Truman
May 9:	Candice Bergen Billy Joel
May 10:	Fred Astaire Bono
May 11:	Irving Berlin Salvador Dali

May 12:	Burt Bacharach George Carlin
May 13:	Joe Louis Peter Gabriel
May 14:	David Byrne George Lucas
May 15:	George Brett Eddy Arnold
May 16:	Janet Jackson Henry Fonda
May 17:	Sugar Ray Leonard Dennis Hopper
May 18:	Reggie Jackson Frank Capra
May 19:	Glenn Close Malcolm X
May 20:	Cher Adolf Hitler
May 21:	Mr. T Peggy Cass
May 22:	Mary Cassatt Laurence Olivier

27

The Gemini Personality: "Talk to Me"

Watch the Twins at a party (where you're bound to
meet them). They stop in on every conversation,
agree with one group that the Republicans are to blame
for the sorry state of the economy, agree with the next
that the Democrats have gotten us into a fine
economic mess, ask the band if they can sit in for a set,
flirt with the hostess, chat with the waitress,
discuss martinis with the bartender.

It tires you out just to *watch* as they spin and whirl.

You want to beg the Twins to stop, *please,*
concentrate on one thing at a time. They can't.
They *need* to show off the little they know about
so many things and find out what other people know,
how they know it, why they know it.

Geminis are the communicators. They scatter their
talent and their wit across the globe. They squeal with
delight at new and stimulating information
before they scatter that around, too.

Remember, there are *two* people inside that
lively body. Both are constantly demanding change,
variety, mental turn-ons. You can almost *see* the two sides
fighting as they chatter at you, rip their napkin
into shreds, and chain smoke.

Then, in a flash, the Twins are gone.
Someone *new* has walked in. They might have
something *fascinating* to relate.

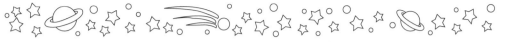

The Gemini Friend

Charmers and flirts, the Twins are always surrounded by
people. It's not easy to break through the crowd and get
close to them. To tell the truth, they have few real friends.
Shallow Gemini backs off when it gets too deep.

Geminis need stimulating friends who share their
weird interests. It's tough to keep up with them.
They attract spirited people who understand why they're
constantly late for appointments (they have *so much* to do)
and join them on a spur-of-the-moment trips
to Egypt to study hieroglyphics.

31

The Gemini Lover

What is love? Why do we love? Are the Twins in love or is this a karmic connection from a past life? These are questions a Gemini will pick through, ponder–and put off when the next, more interesting person comes along. Gadfly Geminis can't shut off their minds and let their hearts take over.

Affairs of the heart just aren't that important to fickle Gemini. Their overworked minds confuse monogamy with *boredom* (their biggest fear). They need freedom. To win their hearts, you must constantly entertain them, seduce them with your wit, intelligence and non-stop mental stimulation, and allow them to be what they are–*confusing*.

An Astrological Compatibility Guide

Gemini and Aries: Like two kids in Candyland, they skip off hand
in hand, convinced they can rule the world.
A beautiful fantasy for them. Scary for the rest of the world.
Anything can happen.

Gemini and Taurus: Routine gives Gemini the jitters.
Routine gives Taurus hot flashes. The only thing the Bull can rely
on is the Twins' unreliability. A rotten idea.

Gemini and Gemini: They encourage each other's weird endeav-
ors, talk until dawn, and team up against boredom.
But two Geminis can uselessly scatter their energy (which is con-
siderable, considering there are four people here) to the winds.

Gemini and Cancer: Childlike Gemini is drawn to Cancer, the eternal mother. Gemini has a lot to learn from Cancer, and sometimes needs shelter under the Crab's shell. Still, the Twins don't deal well with the Crab's possessive streak.

Gemini and Leo: Talk about a challenge. The Twins are adaptable enough to put up with the Lion's boasting, and appreciate his fierce protection. This works better between a female Gemini and male Leo.

Gemini and Virgo: Geminis are children who refuse to grow up. Virgos were born with middle-aged minds. This relationship would take a lot of work, and even more compromise. Best avoided.

Gemini with Libra: A match made in heaven. Libra offers mercurial Gemini mental challenge and freedom. They are soul mates and playmates. Both love people, parties, and ethereal philosophical discussions. A keeper.

Gemini and Scorpio: These two may be drawn to each other in some twisted, masochistic way, but the match-up will lead to heartache. Scorpio is deep, Gemini shallow— and that just scratches the surface.

Gemini and Sagittarius: These two have loud, boisterous fun together. They're a riot to be around. The Twins and the Archer complement each other and spur each other to greater heights.

Gemini and Capricorn: The practical Goat will never, _ever_ understand how the scattered Twins run their unplanned, unpredictable lives. The two can learn a lot from each other—but they might kill each other first.

Gemini and Aquarius: These two understand the weird and wonderful mysteries of each other's minds (if no one else can). Together, they buzz around in a magical wonderland that few earthlings ever reach.

Gemini and Pisces: The differences between these two are, to say the least, overwhelming. Lighthearted Gemini will stomp all over deep Pisces' fragile emotions. End it before the Fish gets hurt (or murders the Twins).

Happy Birthday, Gemini

Buy the Twins anything, and they'll jump around
in delight. They're not picky—as long as it's something *new*
to play with. They'll forget all about your gift
within the hour. (Don't be offended–
it's just that something *else* came along.)

Geminis like green, yellow and bright, vibrant colors. Dull
beige and gray make them nervous. Give them a grab-bag
full of lots of different presents (the weirder, the better).
They live for variety. Satisfy their minds with books
and magazine subscriptions.

Flowers: Lily-of-the-valley, lavender, and myrtle.

Jewels: Agate. It's inexpensive and comes in many colors and designs. Agate brings wisdom, eloquence and protection from accidents.

Clothing: The Twins need lots of clothes—a different outfit for every mood. Anything goes.

Colors: Yellow and purple.

Food: Geminis graze on nuts, leafy vegetable and fruits.

Throw A Party: A surprise party —what else? Geminis live for surprises. Invite lots and lots of different kinds of people and have lots and lots of delightful games and activities planned. Invite an organ grinder and serve something strange, like corn ice cream.

Birthday Directory

(Other Geminis of Fame and Fortune)

May 23:	Douglas Fairbanks Marvin Hagler	June 2:	Stacey Keach Jerry Mathers ("The Beaver")
May 24:	Queen Victoria Bob Dylan	June 3:	Josephine Baker Bert Lance
May 25:	Marshall Tito Miles David	June 4:	Bruce Dern Howard Metzenbaum
May 26:	John Wayne Sally Ride	June 5:	Kenny G Bill Moyers
May 27:	Vincent Price Henry Kissinger	June 6:	Bjorn Borg Dana Carvey
May 28:	Ian Fleming Gladys Knight	June 7:	Prince Rocky Graziano
May 29:	John F. Kennedy Bob Hope	June 8:	Barbara Bush Joan Rivers
May 30:	Mel Blanc Benny Goodman	June 9:	Michael J. Fox Johnny Depp
May 31:	Clint Eastwood Brooke Shields	June 10:	Judy Garland Prince Philip
June 1:	Marilyn Monroe Andy Griffith	June 11:	Vince Lombardi Jacques Cousteau

June 12:	David Rockefeller George Bush
June 13:	Richard Thomas Malcolm McDowell
June 14:	Donald Trump Boy George
June 15:	Waylon Jennings Jim Belushi
June 16:	Roberto Duran Stan Laurel
June 17:	Barry Manilow Dean Martin
June 18:	Paul McCartney Roger Ebert
June 19:	Guy Lombardo Lou Gehrig
June 20:	Cyndi Lauper Bob Vila
June 21:	Jean-Paul Sartre Prince William

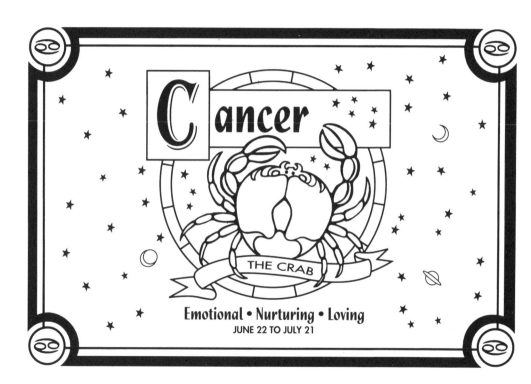

Cancer

THE CRAB

Emotional • Nurturing • Loving
JUNE 22 TO JULY 21

The Cancer Personality: "Love Me"

"Give me your tired, your poor, your downtrodden..."
Yep. The good old U.S. of A. is a Cancer, and the
motherly Statue of Liberty says it all. Crabs want to
protect and save the world. Don't mess with them.
They're fierce. They defend their rights, and the rights
of their friends and family, at any cost.

Male and female, Crabs are the ultimate mothers.
Cancer is the sign of home, mom, and apple pie.

Crabs are intuitive (even psychic) and wear their
emotions like a set of clothes. They're ruled by the moon.
Cancer moods change as it waxes and wanes.
They're laughing one minute, gushing and crying and
getting all sentimental about the weirdest things the next.

Don't ever, *ever* suggest that a Crab get rid of some
of that stuff that's been in the attic for decades. Why,
that spool is from the thread that their great-great
grandmother used to make her wedding dress.
Have you no feeling for *history?*

Cancers adore history, and they remember *everything*.
Ask them about their first day of school (if you have
a lot of time to spare). They'll remember every detail,
down to the cute little socks they wore and the moment
when their mother (sob) actually *left them there.*

Cancers have an unnatural attachment to their mothers.
The fact that Mom left them alone with all those
strangers might be the reason that they're
so emotional and *sensitive* to this day.

The Cancer Friend

A friend in need is a friend indeed. Cancers will always come to your rescue. Crabs can't say no, even if you ask them to carry 150 pounds of luggage on their back up steep hills and through the desert. They smother their pals, but that's only because they *care* so much. Everyone should have a Cancer friend or two.

In return for everything they do, Crabs expect their friends to be there when their funky depressions hit. If you're not around when they need you, they feel personally rejected.

The Cancer Lover

Crabs mate—for life. Their natural instinct is to have kids—lots —so marriage is a must. Over your first lunch date, a Crab will ask demurely whether you prefer June or December weddings.

Crabs are cuddly and sensual. But they withdraw into their shell and snap with their claws when they feel slighted (and they feel slighted more often than most). They need to know they're No. 1. Treat them gently. Crabs are soft when it comes to love.

An Astrological Compatibility Guide

Cancer and Aries: Rams attack; Crabs retreat.
The two have different ideas about everything from the
meaning of life to buttering toast. A painful match.

Cancer and Taurus: These two have the rare ability to be
soul mates, business partners and lovers—all at once.
A union even Bogey and Bacall would envy.

Cancer and Gemini: Childlike Gemini is drawn to Cancer,
the eternal mother. Gemini has a lot to learn from Cancer,
and sometimes needs shelter under the Crab's shell. Still,
the Twins don't deal well with the Crab's possessive streak.

Cancer and Cancer: Snug as bugs, they will cook gourmet meals on a budget, cry on each other's shoulders, get crazy at the full moon. Two Crabs must beware of retreating from the cold, cruel world altogether.

Cancer and Leo: Extravagant, expansive Lions offend cautious Crabs. The Lion's claws are sharper—they will rip Cancer's vulnerable emotions to shreds. These two can easily destroy each other.

Cancer and Virgo: The Crab and the Virgin form a strong, healing emotional bond. But Cancer's tendency toward smothering can send independent Virgo packing.

Cancer and Libra: A tense match that works better between a Cancer male and Libra female. The Crab's emotions clash with Libra's intellectual approach. Both parties have to really want it.

Cancer and Scorpio: They will communicate without words, share their deepest, darkest secrets, and protect each other from the cruelty of outsiders. A magical union, full of empathy, security and trust.

Cancer and Sagittarius: "I didn't mean to say your new pink sweater is *ugly*," the tactless Archer will say as the Crab cries in the corner. But it's too late. Sagittarius' honesty wounds the supersensitive Crab.

Cancer and Capricorn: The super-achieving Goat provides all the security Crabs need—for a price. Capricorns may not have time to meet Cancer's heavy emotional needs. A solid union that requires effort.

Cancer and Aquarius: Aquarius has a lot to offer, but not anything Cancer is looking for. Aquarians are freedom-loving, unconventional and intellectual. Cancers are not. An unlikely pair.

Cancer with Pisces: Great sex. It will sweep away the Fish and the Crab like a tidal wave. Pisces listens with real sympathy to Cancer's changing moods. Both tend toward overindulgence in alcohol, drugs and escapism.

Happy Birthday, Cancer

Don't forget the card—as sappy and mushy as
you can bear. Cover it with X's and O's and tell them
how much you love them a few hundred times.
That oughta make the Crab spill a few of those
sentimental tears that make them look so...*sweet.*

Give Cancers something for their home: candles,
kitchenware, an old-fashioned quilt or embroidered
pillow. Crabs go crazy over antiques. A family
heirloom will send them to the moon with ecstasy.

Flowers: Lilies and white roses.

Jewels: Pearl. Pearls bring patience, purity, and faithfulness. (Note: when you give pearls, make the receiver give you a penny. Otherwise, say the gypsies, pearls bring tears.)

Clothing: Cancers like romantic clothing: shawls and antique jewelry.

Colors: Violet, smoky gray, and silvery blue.

Food: Cancer foods are milk, fish, cabbage, and turnips.

Throw A Party: Gather the family for a big, traditional old-fashioned dinner. Set the table with Grandmother's china and Great Aunt Gertrude's silver. Let the Crab tell stories about birthdays past and take lots of photographs they can cherish later. Play "As Time Goes By."

Birthday Directory

(Other Crabs of Fame and Fortune)

June 22:	Meryl Streep Rose Kennedy	July 2:	Franz Kafka Hermann Hesse	July 12:	Richard Simmons Bill Cosby
June 23:	Clarence Thomas Alfred Kinsey	July 3:	Ken Russell Tom Cruise	July 13:	Cheech Harrison Ford
June 24:	Mick Fleetwood Jack Dempsey	July 4:	Calvin Coolidge Louis Armstrong	July 14:	Ingmar Bergman Gerald Ford
June 25:	Jimmy Walker George Michael	July 5:	P.T. Barnum Huey Lewis	July 15:	Linda Ronstadt Brigitte Nielsen
June 26:	Pearl Buck Peter Lorre	July 6:	Nancy Reagan The Dalai Lama	July 16:	Mary Baker Eddy Ginger Rogers
June 27:	Bob Keeshan ("Captian Kangaroo") H. Ross Perot	July 7:	Ringo Starr Pierre Cardin	July 17:	Phyllis Diller James Cagney
June 28:	Mel Brooks Henry VIII	July 8:	John D. Rockefeller Nelson Rockefeller	July 18:	Hunter S. Thompson Nelson Mandela
June 29:	Fred Grandy Bob Evans	July 9:	Tom Hanks O.J. Simpson	July 19:	Lizzie Borden Duchess of Windsor
June 30:	Mike Tyson Cloris Leachman	July 10:	Arthur Ashe David Brinkley	July 20:	Natalie Wood Carlos Santana
July 1:	Dan Aykroyd Princess Diana	July 11:	Giorgio Armani Yul Brynner	July 21:	Les Aspin Cat Stevens

Leo

THE LION

Positive • Powerful • Protective
JULY 22 TO AUGUST 22

The Leo Personality: "Worship Me"

King of the jungle? No self-respecting lion would settle for *that*. King of the Universe is more like it, thank you.

Lions, ruled by the sun, expect to rule the world. Just as the earth orbits around the fiery ball, they demand that all earthlings revolve around them. After all, it's for the mere mortals' own good. The world could certainly benefit from Leos' superior organization and leadership.

Affectionate and generous, Leos spread sunshine wherever they go. The Lion's flamboyant, dramatic zest for life is infectious. Leos ooze creativity and have much to teach about art, literature, film, fine cuisine, couture (and on and on). They *need* to be recognized and admired. Lions get what they want.

A few Leos take on the pussycat role. Don't be fooled. The fierce Lion lurks within every Leo. Go ahead and cross one. His roar is loud and frightening, his temper explosive. Fortunately for his subjects, the regal Lion rarely holds a grudge.

The Leo Friend

Lions *need* a big circle of adoring, appreciative admirers. (Other people call these friends. In the animal kingdom, a pack of lions is called a pride.)

Leos win their subjects' hearts with big, extravagant bashes and gifts. It's fun to be a loyal Lion's friend–as long as you're open to advice on how to improve your hairstyle, your home decor, your relationships, your lifestyle (and on and on). Though generous, Leos don't offer this wisdom unselfishly. If *you* look good, they look good. And to Leos, looking good is what life's all about.

The Leo Lover

Want to win a Leo's heart? Fly him to Paris for dinner at a five-star restaurant. After the meal, whisk him off to box seats at the opera—in Rome. Feed him caviar and Dom Perignon as dawn breaks. What? You say you can't afford this royal treatment? Uh-oh.

Leos must be wined, dined and seduced with nothing but the best. They need a lover with charm and devastatingly good looks (someone who makes them look good–and they *already* look better than most). They need to be adored and adorned (with jewels, cashmere, you get the picture...). Isn't that what love's all about?

An Astrological Compatibility Guide

Leo and Aries: Rams and Lions coo over each other
and get hot flashes when they're together.
Even their fierce clashes of strong wills are exciting.

Leo and Taurus: Overbearing Leo will set the Bull to stomping
his feet and tossing his horns. Leo needs the freedom of the
jungle; Bulls need to keep an eye on their cows.
An incompatible combination.

Leo and Gemini: Talk about a challenge. The Twins are adapt-
able enough to put up with the Lion's boasting, and appreciate
his fierce protection. This works better between
a female Gemini and male Leo.

Leo and Cancer: Extravagant, expansive Lions offend cautious Crabs. The Lion's claws are sharper–they will rip Cancer's vulnerable emotions to shreds. These two can easily destroy each other.

Leo and Leo: They'll protect, adore and pamper each other— a king and a queen lording over the fiefdom. Lovemaking will be royal bliss. Their clashes of wills, however, can be deadly. (Ever seen a cat fight?)

Leo and Virgo: A union of extremes. It could be sadomasochistic. (A virgin and a lion? Think about it). It could be magical. (A virgin and a lion? Think about it.) A relationship only for the adventurous.

Leo and Libra: Gentle Libra, terrified of the Lion's fierce temper, will tame the Big Cat with subtle diplomacy. Libra has the breathtaking good looks Lions seek. They will take champagne bubble baths and cuddle between luxurious silk sheets.

Leo and Scorpio: Shudder at the thought. Intense, cool Scorpio controls with silent, withering stares that give loud-mouthed Lions the willies. This is one control game Leo can't win, and Lions hate to lose.

Leo and Sagittarius: Energetic and optimistic, Leos and Sagittarians will travel the seven seas and offer each other all the excitement they can stand (a lot). The Archer's occasional arrows of honesty can wound the Lion's pride.

Leo and Capricorn: Lions would delight in spending
all that money practical Goats have saved up for a rainy day–but
no Goat would let them near it. Leos don't believe in rainy days;
Capricorns always carry an umbrella.
Their differences are immense.

Leo and Aquarius: Aquarians are interested in others;
Leos in themselves. The Water Bearer's thoughts are too
far out there to think about personal *appearances.*
Lions think about little else.

Leo and Pisces: This can get confusing, especially if you equate
great sex with love. Pisces doesn't mind–in fact, enjoys–being
dominated by bossy Leo, but the Fish's fits of dark
depression won't be well-received.

Happy Birthday, Leo

The Lion's gift better be big, and it better be luxurious–
with a capital L, for Leo.

Lions *adore* extravagance. Gold–the 24-karat kind and nothing less–makes the Big Cats purr with delight. Don't try to
fool them with that gold-plated stuff. Leos know the
difference. If you can't afford the precious metal, wrap their
gift in gold paper. Tie it up with a big red bow.

A rich meal in a posh restaurant, theater tickets
and a spectacular night on the town should
accompany the material goods.

Flowers: Sunflowers, marigolds and gladiolas.

Jewels: Ruby. It stands for loyalty, charity, and courage. It's expensive.

Clothing: Lions like glamorous, expensive clothes—damasks and velvets please their royal taste.

Colors: Red, orange, gold, and yellow.

Food: Lions are meat eaters. Other foods associated with them are rice and honey.

Throw A Party: Book the most opulent, prestigious place in town (or out of town). Invite their many adoring fans and admirers and put out a spread fit for a king. Hire an orchestra. Give everybody a chance to toast the Lion.

Birthday Directory

(Other Lions of Fame and Fortune)

July 22:	Alex Trebek Don Henley	Aug. 2:	James Baldwin Carroll O'Connor	Aug. 12:	Jane Wyatt George Hamilton
July 23:	Don Drysdale Vincent Sardi, Jr.	Aug. 3:	Tony Bennett Martin Sheen	Aug. 13:	Fidel Castro Alfred Hitchcock
July 24:	Amelia Earhart Linda Carter	Aug. 4:	Roger Clemens John Landis	Aug. 14:	Danielle Steel Earvin "Magic" Johnson
July 25:	Walter Brennan Adnan Khashoggi	Aug. 5:	Loni Anderson Neil Armstrong	Aug. 15:	Princess Anne Julia Child
July 26:	Mick Jagger Carl Jung	Aug. 6:	Lucille Ball Andy Warhol	Aug. 16:	Madonna Timothy Hutton
July 27:	Norman Lear Peggy Fleming	Aug. 7:	Mata Hari Grandma Moses	Aug. 17:	Mae West Sean Penn
July 28:	Jacqueline Kennedy Onassis Richard Rodgers	Aug. 8:	Deborah Norville Dustin Hoffman	Aug. 18:	Patrick Swayze Robert Redford
July 29:	Elizabeth Dole Benito Mussolini	Aug. 9:	Melanie Griffith Whitney Houston	Aug. 19:	Bill Clinton Coco Chanel
July 30:	Arnold Schwartzenegger Henry Ford	Aug. 10:	Rosanna Arquette Herbert Hoover	Aug. 20:	Connie Chung Robert Plant
July 31:	Milton Friedman Julie Giesen	Aug. 11:	Joe Jackson Rev. Jerry Falwell	Aug. 21:	Count Basie Kenny Rogers
Aug. 1:	Yves Saint Laurent Jerry Garcia			Aug. 22:	Norman Schwarzkopf Valerie Harper

Virgo

THE VIRGIN

Receptive • Logical • Thoughtful
AUGUST 23 TO SEPTEMBER 22

The Virgo Personality: "Put Me To Work"

Want to really get to a Virgin? Pick your nose
or swear loudly in public. Throw your jacket on the floor
when you visit. Watch them cringe.

Think of the *Odd Couple's* Felix Unger—meticulous,
nitpicky, constantly worried about his delicate sinuses.
All Virgos aren't *that* bad, of course. But they come close.
They have a deep need for order. When everything's
not just so, they get nauseous.

Virgos didn't earn their reputation as finicky perfectionists for nothing. They nag. It's not that they think they're perfect. Deep inside they know they aren't, and that's what really bothers them. They figure they can make up for their own faults by making *you* perfect.

They're shy at first, but once you get Virgos talking they don't stop. Their inquiring minds want to *know,* and they retain everything. They love to show off their verbal and mental superiority in a good argument–a very *polite* one, of course. The Virgin's favorite phrases are "please," "thank you," and "excuse me."

Virgins have a deep need to be of service to the world—
to feel *useful.* They don't easily take the lead, but any
task you give them will be completed neatly
and perfectly. They would be mortified
to do it any other way.

The whole concept of relaxation throws them.
Even their free time is structured into careful little time
segments–rest from 3 to 3:30, read from 3:30 to 4,
listen to music from 4 to 4:30. (And then for the
fun part–organizing the refrigerator until 5.)

The Virgo Friend

If you don't take their helpful little criticisms personally,
Virgos are excellent pals. They're snooty–they won't hook
up with just *anybody*–but their friendship is worth earning.
Virgos will get you out of jail at 2 in the morning or pick up
your Aunt Alice at dawn. They stick to their promises.

Quiet, gentle Virgos have few enemies. Even when they're
annoyed, they're polite about it. They don't expect a lot out
of people. If you're rude or inconsiderate to them, they
shrug and chalk it up to your basic defects as
a member of the human race.

The Virgo Lover

Virgins are shy (what else would Virgins be?)
when it comes to love. They take it *very* seriously.

Virgos want love more than anything else they can
think of—but not many people meet their incredibly high
standards. Should someone come close, they might
overlook the fact that they squeeze the toothpaste from the
top or don't fold their underwear. But they can't help
offering gentle reminders that this is not proper behavior.

Virgos have a tough time expressing what's in their heart.
They fear the L-word. They don't use it lightly.

An Astrological Compatibility Guide

Virgo and Aries: Rams are fiery, flighty and despise practical people. Virgos are practical people. Bad idea.

Virgo and Taurus: Both are practical, earthy, principled. This is a sensible, stable union likely to result in a house in the suburbs and 2.5 kids.

Virgo and Gemini: Geminis are children who refuse to grow up. Virgos were born with middle-aged minds. This relationship would take a lot of work, and even more compromise. Best avoided.

Virgo and Cancer: This union will make for a strong, healing emotional bond. But Cancer's tendency toward smothering can send Virgo packing.

Virgo and Leo: A union of extremes. It could be sadomasochistic. (A virgin and a lion? Think about it.) It could be magical (A virgin and a lion? Think about it.) This is a relationship only for the adventurous.

Virgo and Virgo: They will try to make each other perfect. They will drive each other crazy. If both can learn to relax, they might not destroy each other.

Virgo and Libra: Libras' intelligence appeals to Virgos. They respect each other. But in the end, the Virgin's realism will deflate Libra's airy charm. A touchy match-up.

Virgo and Scorpio: The Scorpion's protection makes the Virgin feel safe and secure. But the relationship lacks lasting passion, and Scorpios will not tolerate criticism of any kind. Virgos criticize–they can't help it.

Virgo and Sagittarius: An odd match that *can* work. Opposites often attract–and these two can teach and mellow each other. Still, they are very different, and a lot of heartache can be involved.

Virgo and Capricorn: A perfect union, based on mutual understanding and respect. These earthy souls will laugh, cry, and grow old together.

Virgo and Aquarius: Shared intellectual pursuits will draw these two together, but it is best that they remain friends. Aquarius loves the Virgin's mind but has no patience for her emotions. Sexually, the relationship lacks chemistry.

Virgo and Pisces: The Fish lives in the chaos of his vivid imagination. Virgo has no tolerance for poetic nonsense. The differences are entirely too great to make a relationship work.

Happy Birthday, Virgo

Keep it simple. Extravagant gifts make Virgos nervous.
They don't want you to make a big fuss over them.
They find ostentatious displays crass.

Feed their heads. Give them magazine subscriptions (a
scientific or medical journal of some sort), self-help or
analytic psychology books, a calculator or computer
game. Virgins like natural fibers. A basket filled with natural foods is sure to be a hit with health-conscious Virgos.

Flowers: Aster, brightly colored, small flowers.

Jewels: Sapphire. It gives its wearer peace and humility. It symbolizes truth, loyalty and justice.

Clothing: Virgos like fabrics with small, detailed patterns.

Colors: Green, brown and dark blue.

Food: Virgos are health freaks. They like root vegetables, whole foods and all-natural stuff. Many are vegetarians.

Throw A Party: Don't make a big fuss—just make it perfect. Invite the Virgin's loyal friends for a serene candlelit dinner. Hire the best caterer in town to make sure everything is *just* so. Serve poached salmon (no butter), steamed vegetables, and carrot cake.

Birthday Directory

(Other Virgins of Fame and Fortune)

Aug. 23:	Shelley Long	
	Gene Kelly	
Aug. 24:	Gerry Cooney	
	Marlee Matlin	
Aug. 25:	Elvis Costello	
	Sean Connery	
Aug. 26:	Geraldine Ferraro	
	Branford Marsalis	
Aug. 27:	Mother Teresa	
	Pee Wee Herman	
Aug.28:	Ron Guidry	
	David Soul	
Aug. 29:	Michael Jackson	
	Richard Gere	
Aug. 30:	Peggy Lipton	
	Fred MacMurray	
Aug. 31:	Buddy Hackett	
	Van Morrison	
Sept. 1:	Conway Twitty	
	Ann Richards	
Sept. 2:	Jimmy Connors	
	Mark Harmon	

Sept. 3:	Charlie Sheen
	Alan Ladd
Sept. 4:	Paul Harvey
	Dick York
Sept. 5:	Bob Newhart
	Racquel Welch
Sept. 6:	Jane Curtin
	Joseph Kennedy
Sept. 7:	Buddy Holly
	Samuel Goldwyn, Jr.
Sept. 8:	Freddie Mercury
	Sam Nunn
Sept. 9:	Col. Harland Sanders
	Michael Keaton
Sept. 10:	Jose Feliciano
	Arnold Palmer
Sept. 11:	Tom Landry
	Brian Depalma
Sept. 12:	H.L. Mencken
	Margaret Hamilton

Sept. 13:	Jacqueline Bisset
	Claudette Colbert
Sept. 14:	Raymond Floyd
	Joey Heatherton
Sept. 15:	Agatha Christie
	Oliver Stone
Sept. 16:	Lauren Bacall
	J.C. Penney
Sept. 17:	Robert DeNiro
	Warren Burger
Sept. 18:	Frankie Avalon
	Greta Garbo
Sept. 19:	Twiggy
	Mike Royko
Sept. 20:	Sophia Loren
	Jelly Roll Morton
Sept. 21:	Bill Murray
	Stephen King
Sept. 22:	Tommy Lasorda
	Joan Jett

Libra

THE SCALES

Giving • Restless • Trustworthy
SEPTEMBER 23 TO OCTOBER 23

The Libra Personality: "Be Fair With Me"

Got a few hours? Ask a Libra if he would like chocolate or vanilla ice cream. He'll consider. He *likes* chocolate, alright, but if he had vanilla he could put hot fudge on top and have the best of both. But that would be twice as bad for him (and Librans, known for their sweet tooths, have to watch that paunch). Then again, just chocolate is boring, although not as boring as plain old vanilla...

Better yet, don't ask a Libra if he wants chocolate or vanilla ice cream. *Tell* him which kind to have.

Libras just can't make up their minds. It comes from their need to see justice done and their ability to see both sides of *every* issue. They think everything through so thoroughly it's a wonder they ever get out of the house in the morning. Should they wear the blue shirt or red? Loafers or boots? You get the picture.

Libras are the natural judges of the Zodiac. They are fair to all people at all costs. Injustice of any sort (whether to themselves or others) offends them greatly. They argue, naturally, because they can see both sides. But they never get ugly about it.

Ugliness, of any sort, upsets the balance of Libra's delicate Scales. They appreciate fine art and music and beautiful people. In fact, most Libras are beautiful people. They have pretty dimples and dazzling smiles, and they're always dressed to perfection. (You would be, too, if you took that long deciding what to wear).

Libras are often accused of being lazy. That's just not fair (and Libras are *always* fair). They do tend to put off tasks for as long as possible, but once they get going they work quickly and efficiently.

The Libra Friend

Libras hate to be alone. They need someone by their side to share the world's wonders. They need someone to take the other side in those philosophical arguments (oh, sorry... *discussions*) they love so much. They have lots of friends.

Libran friends are loyal and true (the only *fair* way to be). They're charmers. They throw fabulous parties and lavish their buddies with the best. They babysit your kids (and look forward to it), chat over the phone for hours when you can't sleep, and take care of your cat when you're out of town (even if they're allergic to it).

The Libra Lover

Libra is ruled by Venus, the Goddess of Love. If you are blessed with a Libran lover, look to the heavens and thank her for this gentle, affectionate creature.

Libras are sentimental and romantic. They bring you red roses when you're feeling blue and serve you breakfast in bed. Libras love to be in love. It's what they live for. Once in awhile they start petty little arguments. They only do it to make sure you still love them.

An Astrological Compatibility Guide

Libra and Aries: Gentle Libra is among the few who can soften the excitable Ram. Libra respects the Ram's *cahones*. Opposites can attract. But it takes a lot of work.

Libra and Taurus: Libra's flirting will drive Taurus crazy. Libra yawns at the Bull's routines. Both signs appreciate the arts. Limit the relationship to monthly trips to the museum.

Libra and Gemini: A match made in heaven. Libra gives Gemini the mental challenge and freedom the Twins crave. They are soul mates. Both love people, parties, and ethereal philosophical discussions. A keeper.

Cancer and Libra: A tense match that works better between a Cancer male and Libra female. The Crab's emotions clash with Libra's intellectual approach. Both parties have to really want it.

Leo and Libra: Gentle Libra, terrified of the Lion's fierce temper, will tame the Big Cat with subtle diplomacy. Libra has the breathtaking good looks Lions seek. They will take champagne bubble baths and cuddle between luxurious silk sheets.

Libra and Virgo: Libras' intelligence appeals to Virgos. They respect each other. But in the end, the Virgin's realism will deflate Libra's airy charm. A touchy match-up.

Libra and Libra: Perfect harmony. They will talk through the night, cuddle under satin sheets, read poetry to each other. There's more affection and mental stimulation than sexual chemistry, but it all (of course) balances out.

Libra and Scorpio: Scorpio has a lot to teach Libra and is drawn to the Scales in a fatherly way. But Scorpio, who sees only one side to every issue _(his)_, will be sorely tested by Libra's indecision.

Libra and Sagittarius: They share the gift of gab, a love of romantic adventure and the lofty search for truth. Libra and Sagittarius will swashbuckle their way to the land of happily ever after (wherever that may be).

Libra and Capricorn: Capricorn sees the glass half-empty, Libra sees it half-full. The Goat steadily plods the path toward his goal; Libra studies, weighs and agonizes over which path to take. Usually, their paths run in opposite directions (a blessing for both).

Libra and Aquarius: Libra needs peace, harmony— everything smooth and easy. Eccentric Aquarians bump and bruise their delicate balance, put their Scales off kilter. But the mental stimulation is electric.

Libra and Pisces: Days of wine and roses. Spurred on by their passion in the bedroom, these two can learn to blend Libra's intellect with the Fish's dreams (*balance,* you know). Both are romantics—and both overindulge.

Happy Birthday, Libra

Libras will act like their birthday really doesn't matter to them—like you shouldn't make a big fuss. It's an act. Deep down, they're dying to tell the newspaper vendor, the traffic cop and the convenience store clerk that today's *their* special day.

Do not let them be alone on their birthday. (Do not let them be alone, ever.) Give them a flowery card (the mushier the better). Send them two dozen long-stem red roses. They like jewelry and French perfume. Take them to the most expensive restaurant you can afford. Pamper them.

Flowers: Roses (the bigger the better), bluebells and lily-of-the-valley.

Jewels: Opal. It brings friendship, happy marriage and legal success.

Clothing: Libras like comfortable but creative clothing, a bit offbeat or romantic.

Colors: Blue (deep indigo), pink and pale green.

Food: Most Libras are chocoholics. Try not to feed their weakness for sweets. They need natural sugar from fruits and plenty of protein.

Throw A Party: Libras have an inborn need to socialize. Fill a beautifully decorated banquet hall with all their friends. Serve a big, rich chocolate cake. Let them eat all they want of it (it *is*, after all, their birthday). Top off the evening with champagne and strawberries (dipped in more chocolate).

Birthday Directory
(Other Scales of Fame and Fortune)

Sept. 23:	Bruce Springsteen Ray Charles	Oct. 4:	Susan Sarandon Charlton Heston	Oct. 14:	Roger Moore Dwight Eisenhower
Sept. 24:	Jim Henson Joseph P. Kennedy	Oct. 5:	Bob Geldof Vaclav Havel	Oct. 15:	Sarah, Duchess of Yo Lee Iacocca
Sept. 25:	Michael Douglas Barbara Walters	Oct. 6:	Hafez al Assad Britt Ekland	Oct. 16:	Suzanne Somers Angela Lansbury
Sept. 26:	Jack LaLanne Bryan Ferry	Oct. 7:	John Cougar Mellencamp Oliver North	Oct. 17:	Evel Knievel Jimmy Breslin
Sept. 27:	Meat Loaf Shaun Cassidy	Oct. 8:	Rona Barrett Chevy Chase	Oct. 18:	Lee Harvey Oswald Jesse Helms
Sept. 28:	Brigitte Bardot Ed Sullivan	Oct. 9:	John Lennon Jackson Browne	Oct. 19:	Jack Anderson Jennifer Holliday
Sept. 29:	Bryant Gumbel Gene Autry	Oct. 10:	Thelonious Monk Martina Navitrolova	Oct. 20:	Dr. Joyce Brothers Mickey Mantle
Sept. 30:	Angie Dickinson Truman Capote	Oct. 11:	Daryl Hall Eleanor Roosevelt	Oct. 21:	Carrie Fisher Dizzy Gillespie
Oct. 1:	Julie Andrews Jimmy Carter	Oct. 12:	Luciano Pavarotti Adam Rich	Oct. 22:	Brian Boitano Michael Crichton
Oct. 2:	Mahatma Gandhi Sting	Oct. 13:	Lenny Bruce Art Garfunkel	Oct. 23:	Johnny Carson Weird Al Yankovic
Oct. 3:	Charles Bronson Dave Winfield				

Scorpio

THE SCORPION

Secretive • Inquiring • Confident
OCTOBER 24 TO NOVEMBER 22

The Scorpio Personality: "Don't Tread on Me"

C'mon, admit it. When someone tells you they're
a Scorpio, you get a little scared. A slight chill takes
over you. You back away, slowly. You're careful about
what you say. You don't want to offend them.

Maybe it's those deep, penetrating Scorpio eyes,
or that reserved, *chilly* exterior they wear so well.
Whatever it is, you don't want to mess with the Scorpion.
You're sure to lose–painfully.

Scorpio's magnetism is majestic and powerful.
It's the only sign in the Zodiac that has *two* symbols–
the stinging Scorpion and the soaring Eagle. More U.S.
presidents were born under Scorpio than any other sign.
They get what they want, and they use any means to
get it. It's not in your best interest to get in their way.

They're sharp. They're shrewd. They're sly. Be careful
what you tell them. If you offend them, they'll use it later–
years later–to get even. They like to watch others suffer.
It makes them feel powerful.

Everything about Scorpio is mysterious and seductive.
You just *know* they're guarding some incredible secret.
Don't even think about trying to dig it out.
Scorpios don't share secrets. Ever.

They would die if you knew it, but Scorpios have
a weakness. They overindulge in food, sex, drugs
and alcohol. It's the one thing they can't control. It makes
them crazy. (The enlightened ones – the Eagles –
overcome this through spiritual awakening.)

The Scorpio Friend

No one is a better friend or a worse enemy than the Scorpion.
They either love you or hate you – *immediately*. They screen
and scrutinize before they grant friendship.

They like sharp people who stimulate their minds.
If you make the cut, loyal Scorpio is yours for life (and it's
good to have them on your side). They expect total trust.
They want to know where you'll be at 3:00 today and
who you'll be spending next Tuesday with. They won't
tell you their own plans. Don't ask.

If you betray them, they will cut you off immediately. Don't
bother to seek forgiveness. It won't be granted.

The Scorpio Lover

Scorpios get what they want. If they've fixed those sexy, penetrating eyes on you, just lay down and enjoy it. They will have you.

Quite frankly, you should feel honored. Scorpios hate to lose control, and usually hide their emotions under a cool mask. They'll assess the odds and assess *you* quite thoroughly before making a move.

They're highly sexual. They're secretive, possessive and jealous. Don't even *look* at another. When scorned, Scorpions are vindictive and cruel – murder is not out of the question.

An Astrological Compatibility Guide

Scorpio and Aries: Danger. Rams demand to be the aggressor. Scorpions demand to be the aggressor. Scorpions love secrets. Rams can't keep them. Stand clear.

Scorpio and Taurus: The most divine enemies in the Zodiac. They admire and envy each other, but would rather die than admit it. Run, don't walk, from this fatal attraction.

Scorpio and Gemini: These two may be drawn to each other in some twisted, masochistic way, but the match-up will lead to heartache. Scorpio is deep, Gemini shallow— and that just scratches the surface.

Scorpio and Cancer: They will communicate
without words, share their deepest, darkest secrets,
and protect each other from the cruelty of outsiders.
A magical union, full of empathy, security and trust.

Scorpio and Leo: Shudder at the thought. Intense,
cool Scorpio controls with silent, withering stares that give
loud-mouthed Lions the willies. This is one control game
Leo can't win, and Lions *hate* to lose.

Scorpio and Virgo: The Scorpion's protection makes
the Virgin feel safe and secure. But the relationship lacks
lasting passion, and Scorpios will not tolerate criticism
of any kind. Virgos criticize—they can't help it.

Scorpio and Libra: Scorpio has a lot to teach Libra and is drawn to the Scales in a fatherly way. But Scorpio, who sees only one side to every issue *(his)*, will be sorely tested by Libra's indecision.

Scorpio and Scorpio: A powerful emotional roller coaster. Together, they could save, or destroy, the world (and each other). Sex will be a religious experience. A rocky climb to soaring heights that could end suddenly with one false step.

Scorpio and Sagittarius: A combination too scary to consider. Sagittarius, who speaks without thinking, will wound supersensitive Scorpio again and again (a dangerous thing to do). Sag is open and honest; Scorpio feeds on secrets. Lethal.

Scorpio and Capricorn: Scorpio will be pleased and puzzled that the unemotional Goat has little interest in his closely guarded secrets. They will be a "power couple," feeding off each other's drive and ambition. But they will never, ever completely understand each other.

Scorpio and Aquarius: If one thing bugs Scorpio, it's not to understand someone—and *no one* understands Aquarians. Both are curious about people (for different reasons); they'll probe each other's minds and motivations. The results could be enlightening.

Scorpio and Pisces: They understand each other's deep emotions and carry those into the bedroom. A better match between a Pisces woman and Scorpio male, but in general, this has excellent potential.

100

Happy Birthday, Scorpio

Just don't make a big deal of it. Scorpions never actively seek the limelight. It makes them nervous to be the center of attention. They're suspicious of gifts— they wonder what you want in return.

Don't surprise them with something they don't expect. Get them things they can play with, *alone.* They like to entertain themselves in the privacy of their own domain, so a television, VCR or any home-entertainment gadgets will please them. They like sex toys and booze, but those are bad for them.

Flowers: Geraniums, rhododendrons and bright red flowers.

Jewels: Topaz. It brings fidelity (which Scorpions demand) and strength.

Clothing: Scorpios don't like flashy or extreme clothes. Keep it subtle.

Colors: Deep red and maroon, black and purple.

Food: Scorpios like onions, leeks and garlic—strong-tasting foods for their strong wills. They tend to overindulge in food and drink.

Throw A Party: Do *not* throw a surprise party. Do not plan a roast. A nice orgy of food and drink, with the friends and relatives they trust, will suffice. Don't make them squirm while everybody stares and sings "Happy Birthday." Sing it while they're in the bathroom, where they can smile and be pleased—*secretly.*

Birthday Directory

(Other Scorpions of Fame and Fortune)

Oct. 24:	Kevin Kline	Nov. 3:	Roseanne Barr-Arnold	Nov. 13:	Garry Marshall
Oct. 25:	Helen Reddy		Michael Dukakis		Louis Brandeis
	Pablo Picasso	Nov. 4:	Walter Cronkite	Nov. 14:	Prince Charles
Oct. 26:	Mahalia Jackson		Loretta Swit		Mamie Eisenhower
	Jaclyn Smith	Nov. 5:	Ike Turner	Nov. 15:	Georgia O'Keefe
Oct. 27:	Pat Sajak		Paul Simon		Ed Asner
	Theodore Roosevelt	Nov. 6:	Sally Field	Nov. 16:	Lisa Bonet
Oct. 28:	Bruce Jenner		Maria Shriver		Dwight Gooden
	Julia Roberts	Nov. 7:	Joni Mitchell	Nov. 17:	Rock Hudson
Oct. 29:	Kate Jackson		Billy Graham		Lauren Hutton
	Richard Dreyfuss	Nov. 8:	Katharine Hepburn	Nov. 18:	Linda Evans
Oct. 30:	Henry Winkler		Christie Hefner		George Gallup
	Grace Slick	Nov. 9:	Spiro Agnew	Nov. 19:	Jodie Foster
Oct. 31:	John Candy		Carl Sagan		Ted Turner
	Michael Landon	Nov. 10:	Richard Burton	Nov. 20:	Ahmad Rashad
Nov. 1:	Walter Matthau		MacKenzie Phillips		Richard Dawson
	Larry Flint	Nov. 11:	Charles Manson	Nov. 21:	Goldie Hawn
Nov. 2:	Patrick Buchanan		Demi Moore		Mariel Hemingway
	Burt Lancaster	Nov. 12:	Neil Young	Nov. 22:	Rodney Dangerfield
			Nadia Comaneci		Billie Jean King

Sagittarius
THE ARCHER
Exuberant • Enthusiastic • Optimistic
NOVEMBER 23 TO DECEMBER 21

The Sagittarius Personality: "Play With Me"

The symbol for Sagittarius is a funny-looking thing.
It's half Centaur (horse) and half Archer (man). It stands for
man trying to lift himself from his lower nature. Imagine a
man's torso on a horse's hind end, trying to balance and
shoot an arrow. It makes Sag ...well...*clumsy.*

They're forever putting those horse's feet in their mouths.
"I didn't mean you were getting *fat*," they'll say. "Really, I
think those extra twenty pounds look *good* on you. You have
the kind of frame that can carry a lot of extra weight."

Is this an apology, or should you storm out the door?
Give poor Sag a break. He can't help that he's brutally
honest and doesn't know when to shut his mouth.
Happy-go-lucky Sag never *means* any harm. He always
tells the truth. Some people call it tactless.

Sag is ruled by Jupiter, the planet of expansion.
Archers boast a lot and exaggerate a little. Just take what
they say with a grain of salt, and try to get them talking
about something important, like religion or philosophy.
They're very wise in these subjects. They'll talk–
and you'll want to listen–for hours.

The Sagittarius Friend

How can you not like a Sag? They're lively and fun.
They always pick up the dinner tab.

Archers are constantly looking to add new dimensions to
their life. They make friends everywhere, from
the tavern to the grocery store line.

If you can stand it, no one is more fun to be around.
Archers drag you from the hippest new health club to the
hottest night club and plan a weekend trip to the Bahamas
over shots of tequila. They fart and belch and think it's
hilarious. But admit it. It *was* funny (for everyone but Martha)
when he put that whoopee cushion on Martha's chair.

The Sagittarius Lover

Let's get this straight right from the start. Sag *will not tolerate* any restrictions on his personal freedom. If you try to pin him down, he will blow you a kiss and fly off to Buenos Aires. Sag is terrified of responsibility, reluctant to commit, and not crazy about marriage.

Still interested? Be prepared for a wild ride. Archers are looking for someone clever and on-the-go like themselves, a traveling companion as well as lover. They flirt, and sometimes in their quest for adventure, they cheat. Then their honesty gets the best of them, and they tell you about it. Ouch.

An Astrological Compatibility Guide

Sagittarius and Aries: They both believe in Santa Claus, telling the truth even if it hurts, and talking. And talking. And talking. If they can shut up long enough to listen to each other, this match is made in heaven.

Sagittarius and Taurus: Sagittarius lives for adventure; Taurus lives for cozy nights by the fire. Sagittarius can't sit still; Taurus is a lounging pro. A mismatch.

Sagittarius and Gemini: These two have loud, boisterous fun together. They're a riot to be around. The Twins and the Archer complement each other and spur each other to greater heights.

Sagittarius and Cancer: "I didn't mean to say your new pink sweater is *ugly*," the tactless Archer will say as the Crab cries in the corner. But it's too late. Sagittarius' honesty will never fail to wound the supersensitive Crab. And that's just the beginning of their differences.

Sagittarius and Leo: Energetic and optimistic, Leos and Sagittarians will travel the seven seas and offer each other all the excitement they can stand (a lot). But the Archer's occasional arrows of honesty can wound the Lion's pride.

Sagittarius and Virgo: An odd match that can work. Opposites often attract—and these two can teach and mellow each other. Still, they are very different, and a lot of heartache can be involved.

Sagittarius and Libra: They share the gift of gab,
a love of romantic adventure and the lofty search for truth.
Libra and Sagittarius will swashbuckle their way to the land
of happily ever after (wherever that may be).

Sagittarius and Scorpio: A combination too scary to consider.
Sagittarius, who speaks without thinking, will wound
supersensitive Scorpio again and again (a dangerous thing to
do). Sag is open and honest, Scorpio feeds on secrets. Lethal.

Sagittarius and Sagittarius: Their lives together will
be everything—except dull. They will talk, travel, laugh,
learn— all to excess. Jupiter's expansion will take this
relationship beyond their wildest dreams.

Sagittarius and Capricorn: In this case, opposites don't attract—nor should they. The Goat should stay in the safety and comfort of home and wave good-bye to happy-go-lucky Sag as he trots off to Timbuktu. Nothing's worth this kind of heartache.

Sagittarius and Aquarius: They will be best friends as well as lovers, feeding off each other's fine minds and enthusiasm. Sag will sate his wanderlust with a trip into the weird and wonderful mysteries of Aquarius' mind—and find little reason to stray.

Sagittarius and Pisces: The Fish is moody and prone to withdraw in fits of depression; the Archer is optimistic and prone to fits of laughter. The only thing these two have in common is their mutual mismanagement of money.

Happy Birthday, Sagittarius

Have fun—as much as you can stand—celebrating Sag's
birthday. Make everything loud and obnoxious
and throw in a few gag gifts.

Archers like toys—things they can use in their non-stop
on-the-go in-your-face lives: boxing gloves, a tennis racquet,
ski equipment, lift tickets, behind-the-plate seats at Yankee
Stadium (and plane tickets to New York if you don't live there).

Take travel-hungry Sag on a trip to someplace exotic,
like Khartoum. Take him to the track—Sag has naturally
good luck. Sag loves to party. A bottle of booze
(if you'll share it with him) will be a hit.

Flowers: Narcissus, goldenrod and carnations.

Jewels: Turquoise, a symbol of love, protection, freedom and affluence.

Clothing: Activewear–tennis shorts or lycra will please them most.

Colors: Rich purples and blues.

Food: Archers love to party hearty–with rich food and lots of drink. Bulb vegetables, grapefruit, currants and celery are the *healthy* foods associated with them.

Throw A Party: Obnoxious. Hilarious. Out-of-control. Sag won't think it's a success unless the police come. Invite thousands. Hire a clown and a stripper and a polka band. Let him eat a lot and drink a lot and belch and give a loud, overbearing toast to himself.

Birthday Directory

(Other Archers of Fame and Fortune)

Nov. 23:	Billy the Kid Harpo Marx	Dec. 3:	Ozzy Osbourne Andy Williams	Dec. 13:	Tim Conway Ted Nugent
Nov. 24:	William F. Buckley, Jr. Carrie Nation	Dec. 4:	Jeff Bridges Don Hewitt	Dec. 14:	Stan Smith Charlie Rich
Nov. 25:	John F. Kennedy, Jr. Amy Grant	Dec. 5:	Walt Disney Joan Didion	Dec. 15:	J. Paul Getty Don Johnson
Nov. 26:	Charles Schulz Tina Turner	Dec. 6:	Ira Gershwin Agnes Moorehead	Dec. 16:	Margaret Mead Frank Deford
Nov. 27:	Danny DeVito Jimi Hendrix	Dec. 7:	Ted Knight Larry Bird	Dec. 17:	Arthur Fiedler Bob Guccione
Nov. 28:	Gary Hart Randy Newman	Dec. 8:	Kim Basinger Flip Wilson	Dec. 18:	Steven Spielberg Keith Richards
Nov. 29:	Gary Shandling Diane Ladd	Dec. 9:	Kirk Douglas Donny Osmond	Dec. 19:	Jennifer Beals Cicily Tyson
Nov. 30:	Bo Jackson Billy Idol	Dec. 10:	Susan Dey Chet Huntley	Dec. 20:	Gordon Getty Irene Dunne
Dec. 1:	Woody Allen Bette Midler	Dec. 11:	Donna Mills Terri Garr	Dec. 21:	Phil Donahue Frank Zappa
Dec. 2:	Alexander Haig George Seurat	Dec. 12:	Cathy Rigby Ed Koch		

Capricorn

THE GOAT

Determined • Perfectionist • Organized
DECEMBER 22 TO JANUARY 21

The Capricorn Personality: "Do The Right Thing"

Suggest to a Capricorn that the two of you go skinnydipping in the public fountain—just for the heck of it. His ears will turn red. He will shudder. He will look at you like you've lost your marbles.

"That is illegal, immoral, and furthermore" (here he's got you) *"it makes no sense,"* he'll say.

Everything Goats do is legal, moral, and makes sense.
That's why they're so successful. They're shrewd,
methodical, and driven—a corporate dream.
Goats stick with tradition—what worked for their
grandparents is just fine for them, thank you.

Goats plod with determination to the top.
They don't make mistakes. They plan their lives carefully,
from which suit they will wear on Tuesday to which
money-market fund they will invest in. Goats always
have savings to invest. They're thrifty (some call it cheap).
They save the tin foil from carry-out food.

They only talk about important subjects, like the
stock market. They get upset if you know something
they don't about an important subject, like the
stock market. They like to be recognized as the
best at what they do—and they usually are.

Goats *do* learn to relax as they get older. Once they've
accomplished all that they need to (a lot more than most),
they start growing younger. They allow themselves to
indulge in their natural love of nature, art, and music and
nurture their own creativity. They let a little sentiment seep
through their tough shells. They may even buy a puppy.

The Capricorn Friend

Goats tend to be loners. They're afraid to have friends, because they're afraid of being hurt. They carefully select a few intimate friends deserving of their undying loyalty.

Goats take friendship as seriously as they take everything else. They have sturdy shoulders, they keep promises, they're responsible and loyal. Don't cross them, or you're out of their life forever. You don't get a second chance.

Beware of Goats on their way to the top. They can be opportunists, using people in the name of friendship.

The Capricorn Lover

Somewhere under that chilly, reserved exterior,
Goats have a heart. They *have* to. Everybody does.

It ain't easy to find. Goats are shy and cautious when it
comes to love. All that gushy stuff gives them heartburn.

They can get sidetracked by surface virtues—like wealth,
power or social status—and marry for all the wrong
reasons. This can lead to a less-than-happy marriage.
But once they've signed on, most Goats stay married.
They stubbornly believe they can work anything out.

An Astrological Compatibility Guide

Capricorn and Aries: The Ram lives by his wits. The Goat plans out which socks he will wear the night before. Where Capricorn finds peace, Aries finds boredom. Only the sure-footed would attempt this rocky climb.

Capricorn and Taurus: Carefully planned destiny. Their solid love results in a church wedding, well-mannered children, and a fat pension fund. Dan Quayle, eat your heart out. We're talking family values here.

Capricorn and Gemini: The practical Goat will never, ever understand how the scattered Twins run their unplanned, unpredictable lives. The two can learn a lot from each other—but they'll probably kill each other first.

Capricorn and Cancer: The super-achieving Goat provides all the security Crabs need—for a price. Capricorns may not have time to meet Cancer's heavy emotional needs. A solid union that requires effort

Capricorn and Leo: Lions would delight in spending all that money practical Goats have saved up for a rainy day–but no self-respecting Goat would let them near it. Leos don't believe in rainy days; Capricorns always carry an umbrella. Their differences are immense.

Capricorn and Virgo: A perfect union, based on mutual understanding and respect. These earthy souls will laugh, cry, and grow old together.

Capricorn and Libra: Capricorn sees the glass half-empty, Libra sees it half-full. The Goat steadily plods the path toward his goal; Libra studies, weighs and agonizes over which path to take. Usually, their paths run in opposite directions (a blessing for both).

Capricorn and Scorpio: Scorpio will be pleased and puzzled that the unemotional Goat has little interest in his closely guarded secrets. They will be a "power couple," feeding off each other's drive and ambition. But they will never, ever completely understand each other.

Scorpio and Sagittarius: In this case, opposites don't attract—nor should they. The Goat should stay in the safety and comfort of home and wave good-bye to happy-go-lucky Sag as he trots off to Timbuktu. Nothing's worth this kind of heartache.

Capricorn and Capricorn: They'll respect, honor and admire each other. Side by side, they'll build a solid life and substantial savings for a rainy day. Trouble is, they both think too much about that rainy day. This relationship can get gloomy.

Capricorn and Aquarius: It's not the worst combination under the sun—but it comes pretty close. Both sides will have to work very hard to overcome their completely different outlooks and attitudes. If they can do that, they'll learn a lot from each other.

Capricorn and Pisces: On the surface, their differences seem great, but they're softened through natural communication and mutual acceptance. They will spend many warm nights by the fire, away rom the crowds, basking in the sympathetic vibrations of their union.

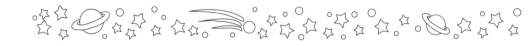

Happy Birthday, Capricorn

Don't buy them a whimsical miniature merry-go-round or something equally stupid. Goats like gifts they can *use*.

Capricorns appreciate prestigious designer names because the stuff is generally made well: a Coach leather briefcase, a Brooks Brothers tie, a Chanel suit. They like books about business (how to succeed in it) and biographies.

Think of the most practical, boring gift you could give. Go out and buy it. The Goat will love it.

Flowers: Poppies, pansies, holly and ivy.

Jewels: Garnet. It brings loyalty, determination and permanence. If the Goat *must* travel, it will protect them.

Clothing: Conservative, traditional clothes fit Goats best.

Colors: Brown, gray, black, dark green, maroon.

Food: Capricorns are meat-and-potato types. Barley, beets, spinach and starchy foods are associated with them.

Throw A Party: Keep it simple. Throw a traditional birthday party with a traditional white cake and traditional candles. Sing the traditional song. Get the idea? Goats really *like* to be the center of attention, so shower them with lots of it. Let them give a solemn speech about all they've accomplished over the years.

Birthday Directory

(Other Goats of Fame and Fortune)

Dec. 22:	Barbara Billingsly Maurice and Robin Gibb
Dec. 23:	Jose Greco Susan Lucci
Dec. 24:	Howard Hughes Ava Gardner
Dec. 25:	Sissy Spacek Jimmy Buffett
Dec. 26:	Carlton Fisk Henry Miller
Dec. 27:	Gerard Depardieu Marlene Dietrich
Dec. 28:	Mao Zedong Woodrow Wilson
Dec. 29:	Mary Tyler Moore Ted Danson
Dec. 30:	Bert Parks Jack Lord
Dec. 31:	Anthony Hopkins Tim Matheson

Jan 1:	Barry Goldwater J. Edgar Hoover
Jan. 2:	Dan Rostenkowski J.R.R. Tolkien
Jan. 3:	Victoria Principal Dabney Coleman
Jan. 4:	Don Shula Jane Wyman
Jan. 5:	Walter Mondale Diane Keaton
Jan. 6:	Rev. Suun Myung Moon Bonnie Franklin
Jan. 7:	Nicolas Cage Kenny Loggins
Jan. 8:	David Bowie Elvis Presley
Jan. 9:	Joan Baez Richard Nixon
Jan. 10:	Pat Benatar George Forman

Jan. 11:	Ben Crenshaw Naomi Judd
Jan. 12:	Kirstie Alley Howard Stern
Jan. 13:	Gary Moore Charles Nelson Reilly
Jan. 14:	Andy Rooney Faye Dunaway
Jan. 15:	Cardinal John O'Connor Martin Luther King, Jr
Jan. 16:	A.J. Foyt Sade
Jan. 17:	Muhammad Ali Betty White
Jan. 18:	Kevin Costner Cary Grant
Jan. 19:	Robert Palmer Janis Joplin
Jan. 20:	Federico Fellini David Lynch
Jan 21:	Wolfman Jack Geena Davis

129

The Aquarius Personality: "Live and Let Live"

Aquarians are not really from here. They were dropped onto Earth by aliens from the planet. They are not like us. They're weird. They like it that way.

Aquarians know how the phases of the moon affect animal psychology and can predict the upcoming scientific discovery of a planet that spins backwards around Jupiter, causing the grass to grow more slowly on Earth. They can communicate with animals and stars. They *know* these things that mere humans do not. Believe it.

Some people think Aquarians are mad (geniuses are always accused of being insane). They don't really care what you think. And they don't spend a lot of time taking *your* inventory, either.

If you live in a cardboard box on a street corner, they'll think it quite *inventive* of you to create a cozy home out of garbage. They'll buy you a cup of coffee and tell you how to tap into energy from the sewer system for heat. They'll wonder if living in garbage might be the next big thing (Aquarians are *always* a step ahead of the rest).

Most of all, they'll leave you feeling all warm and wacky. Aquarius is the sign of brotherly love.

The Aquarius Friend

Aquarians love to meet new people. They might *learn* something—or at least pass along some theories of relativity to a new face. They find something wonderful in everybody. They'll give you their last dime.

Aquarians have lots of friends and few enemies. Their most intimate friends are radical or bohemian, like they are, and give them space to wander the cosmos.

Don't be offended if an Aquarian friend momentarily forgets your name. With all that data banging around in their heads, they can be a bit absent-minded.

The Aquarian Lover

Love's all right. In fact, Aquarians are rather intrigued by the glamour and glimmer of romance. But when it comes right down to it, they value friendship much more highly.

All that flowery language seems a waste of time. Public displays of affection embarrass them (and they don't embarrass easily). While you're wooing them, they're thinking about the theory of astrological order in reincarnation.

A lot of them never marry. They need space to explore. Give it to them. The more freedom you allow them, the more faithful they will be.

An Astrological Compatibility Guide

Aquarius and Aries: Fascinating. Together, they will fight for justice in Khartoum, study Buddhism in Tibet. A powerful union, but the Aquarian's natural interest in (gasp) *others* will miff self-centered Aries.

Aquarius and Taurus: Aquarius moves a step ahead of the rest; Taurus plods slowly with the crowd. Aquarians need detachment; Bulls need devotion. Their differences are so immense they may need a translator to say hello.

Aquarius and Gemini: These two understand the weird and wonderful mysteries of each other's minds (if no one else can). Together, they buzz around in a magical wonderland that few earthlings ever reach.

Aquarius and Cancer: Aquarius has a lot to offer, but not anything Cancer is looking for. Aquarians are freedom-loving, unconventional and intellectual. Cancers are not. An unlikely pair.

Aquarius and Leo: Aquarians are interested in others; Leos in themselves. The Water Bearer's thoughts are too far out there to think about personal *appearances.* Lions think about little else.

Aquarius and Virgo: Shared intellectual pursuits will draw these two together, but it is best that they remain friends. Aquarius loves the Virgin's mind but has no patience for her emotions. Sexually, the relationship lacks chemistry.

Aquarius and Libra: Libra needs peace, harmony—
everything smooth and easy. Eccentric Aquarians bump
and bruise their delicate balance, put their Scales off kilter.
But the mental stimulation is electric.

Aquarius and Scorpio: If one thing bugs Scorpio,
it's not to understand someone—and *no one* understands Aquarians.
Both are curious about people (for different
reasons); they'll probe each other's minds and motivations.
The results could be enlightening.

Aquarius and Sagittarius: They will be best friends as well as lovers,
feeding off each other's fine minds and enthusiasm. Sag will sate his
wanderlust with a trip into the weird and wonderful
mysteries of Aquarius' mind—and find little reason to stray.

Aquarius and Capricorn: It's not the worst combination under the sun—but it comes pretty close. Both sides will have to work very hard to overcome their completely different outlooks and attitudes. If they can do that, they'll learn a lot from each other.

Aquarius and Aquarius: They will be best friends, soul mates, wanderers into the weirdness and wonder of the universe. A match made in heaven (or whatever concept these two explore, debate and decide upon for that bestower of great miracles in the sky).

Aquarius and Pisces: As friends or business associates, these two are a powerful force that could save the world. They share humanitarian concerns. But their emotional incompatibility (the Fish's excess of, the Water Bearer's lack of) can easily destroy a love relationship.

Happy Birthday, Aquarius

It better be bizarre. They'll be miffed at a gift of
underwear or a drugstore card with a pretty verse.

Aquarians like modern gizmos and gadgets—
they're into the highest of high technology.
A super-powered telescope (for watching the stars...
and studying the human psychology of their neighbors),
a supersonic juicer/slicer/dicer, or an X-ray camera
will keep them busy for awhile. Give them stilts (they'll
use them as transportation to the grocery store)
or a book on homeopathic medicine.

Flowers: Orchids, daffodils and primrose.

Jewels: Amethyst, a symbol of sincerity. It brings prophetic ability, poise and self-discipline.

Clothing: Aquarians like offbeat, eccentric clothing. Pick out something you wouldn't be caught dead in. Aquarius will look great in it.

Colors: Electric blue, turquoise, white, yellow and green.

Food: Aquarians like dried fruit and hard-to-find produce like kumquats, kiwi and star fruits. Red hot chili peppers turn them on.

Throw A Party: Along with their huge gaggle of friends, invite kids from the local orphanage or homeless families from the shelter. Aquarians live to help those less fortunate than themselves. They'll want others to benefit from their special day. Serve unexpected food, like kumquat-chocolate tarts. Schedule time for a seance.

Birthday Directory

(Other Water Bearers of Fame and Fortune)

Jan. 22:	Bill Bixby Linda Blair	Feb. 1:	Boris Yeltsin Sherman Hemsley	Feb. 11:	Tina Louise Burt Reynolds
Jan. 23:	Princess Caroline Chita Rivera	Feb. 2:	Farrah Fawcett Garth Brooks	Feb. 12:	Arsenio Hall Joe Garagiola
Jan. 24:	John Belushi Mary Lou Retton	Feb. 3:	Norman Rockwell Morgan Fairchild	Feb. 13:	Stockard Channing George Segal
Jan. 25:	Somerset Maugham Robert Burns	Feb. 4:	Dan Quayle Rosa Parks	Feb. 14:	Florence Henderson Jimmy Hoffa
Jan. 26:	Anita Baker Gene Siskel	Feb. 5:	Hank Aaron Tom Brokaw	Feb. 15:	Harvey Korman Anthony Burgess
Jan. 27:	William Randolph Hearst, Jr. Donna Reed	Feb. 6:	Ronald Reagan Zsa Zsa Gabor	Feb. 16:	John McEnroe Sonny Bono
Jan. 28:	Alan Alda Mikhail Baryshnikov	Feb. 7:	Sinclair Lewis Gay Talese	Feb. 17:	Michael Jordan Hal Holbrook
Jan. 29:	Tom Selleck Oprah Winfrey	Feb. 8:	Gary Coleman Ted Koppel	Feb. 18:	Yoko Ono Vanna White
Jan. 30:	Gene Hackman Phil Collins	Feb. 9:	Mia Farrow Carole King	Feb. 19:	Prince Andrew Smokey Robinson
Jan 31:	Carol Channing Suzanne Pleshette	Feb. 10:	Roberta Flack Mark Spitz	Feb. 20:	Charles Barkley Patty Hearst

Pisces

THE FISH

Imaginative • Impulsive • Intuitive
FEBRUARY 21 TO MARCH 20

141

The Pisces Personality: "Let Me Help You"

Pisces' symbol is two fish, one for the personality and one for the soul. They're swimming in opposite directions. Most Pisces feel like both are swimming upstream. They're troubled. Harsh words or gray weather send them into a deep funk for weeks.

Fish don't expect much out of life. They know they're going to come in last, get the smallest piece of the pie, be overlooked when choosing sides for basketball. They think they deserve it because they've been bad.

Pisces are saints and martyrs. They care *deeply* about everyone else's problems. They're psychic–the vibes around them make them all itchy. They'll do anything to help their friends, but they don't know how to help themselves. It ain't easy being a Fish. They wallow in self-pity and gorge themselves in food, booze or drugs. This makes them more depressed. It's a vicious cycle.

Fish need time alone every day to build up their squeamish energies. Pisces love art and poetry and mystical things. They believe in magic. They're deep.

The Pisces Friend

They'll always remember your birthday. They'll listen to your romantic entanglements until dawn (when everyone else is sick of hearing them). They'll drive you to and from the dentist and hold your hand when you get a root canal.

Pisces live to help their fellow man. Resist the temptation to take advantage of these gentle souls—it's far too easy. They are always there for you. They're friends for life. They will *never* hurt you.

The Pisces Lover

Pisces looks wistfully at the waxing moon and knows that somewhere out there is a soul mate who will accept their adoring gestures, love poems and white roses. *Somewhere.*

That someone won't mind standing up on a pedestal while Pisces gazes affectionately at them through rose-colored glasses. The Fish love to love. They bring their beloved peonies because it's Tuesday, chocolates because it's Friday. They wouldn't mind a few unexpected little somethings in return.

They want to remain friends with their past lovers forever. They believe they'll eventually come to realize what a good thing they had.

An Astrological Compatibility Guide

Pisces and Aries: The Ram will trample all over watery, supersensitive Pisces. The Fish lives in a fantasy world all his own; the Ram knows only reality. A masochistic match, once you get past the sexual chemistry.

Pisces and Taurus: Pisces is a fantasy addict; Taurus a harsh realist. The dreamy Fish's illusions will drive the earthy Bull to murder. A masochistic match-up.

Pisces and Gemini: The differences between the Twins and the Fish are, to say the least, overwhelming. Lighthearted Gemini will stomp all over deep Pisces' fragile emotions. End it before the Fish gets hurt (or murders the Twins).

Pisces and Cancer: Great sex. It will sweep away the Fish and the Crab like a tidal wave. Pisces listens with real sympathy to Cancer's changing moods. Both tend toward overindulgence in alcohol, drugs and escapism.

Pisces and Leo: This can get confusing, especially if you equate great sex with love. Pisces doesn't mind–in fact, enjoys–being dominated by bossy Leo, but the Fish's fits of dark depression won't be well-received.

Pisces and Virgo: The Fish lives in the chaos of his vivid imagination. Virgo has no tolerance for poetic nonsense. The differences are entirely too great to make a relationship work.

Pisces and Libra: Days of wine and roses. Spurred on by their passion in the bedroom, these two can learn to blend Libra's intellect with the Fish's dreams (*balance,* you know). Both are romantics—and both can overindulge.

Pisces and Scorpio: They understand each other's deep emotions and carry those into the bedroom. A better match between a Pisces woman and Scorpio male, but in general, this has excellent potential.

Pisces and Sagittarius: The Fish is moody and prone to withdraw in fits of depression; the Archer is optimistic and prone to fits of laughter. The only thing these two have in common is their mutual mismanagement of money.

Pisces and Capricorn: On the surface, their differences seem great, but they're softened through natural communication and mutual acceptance. They will spend many warm nights by the fire, away from the crowds, basking in the sympathetic vibrations of their union.

Pisces and Aquarius: As friends or business associates, these two are a powerful force that could save the world. They share humanitarian concerns. But their emotional incompatibility (the Fish's excess of, the Water Bearer's lack of) can easily destroy a love relationship.

Pisces and Pisces: They'll look deep into each other's watery eyes and understand without speaking a word. Their communication is sympathetic, intuitive—psychic. But each needs a strong mate to prod them out of despondency. Another Fish might not be the one.

Happy Birthday, Pisces

Make it mystical, magical, and mysterious.

Fish love romance. Stimulate their deep, dreamy side
with candles or incense, a cedar chest of
aromatherapy oils, a crystal ball.

Books about the romantic days of old—dungeons and
dragons, King Arthur—appeal to them. They read poetry,
and actually like it. A CD of classical or pagan music
soothes their senses. A bottle of Benedictine & Brandy or
a soft, velvety robe satisfies their sensual desires.

Flowers: Water lilies, violets and irises.

Jewels: Aquamarine. It protects the wearer from the hazards of the sea and sharpens the intellect.

Clothing: Pisces like flowing, romantic clothes of sensual fabrics like silk or chiffon. Comfort is important.

Colors: Sea green, silver, violet and purple.

Food: Pisces are associated with pumpkin, cucumber, lettuce and melon.

Throw A Party: Candlelight, incense and sensual music set the mood for a Fish feast. Don't throw a big bash. A romantic evening with the one they love suits them just fine. Serve fine wine in gold-plated goblets and passionfruit soufflé. Hire a magician to entertain them, and a fortune teller to predict their year to come.

Birthday Directory

(Other Fish of Fame and Fortune)

Feb. 21: David Geffen Erma Bombeck	**March 1:** Roger Daltry Ron Howard	**March 11:** Sam Donaldson Lawrence Welk
Feb. 22: George Washington Edward Kennedy	**March 2:** Mikhail Gorbachev Dr. Seuss	**March 12:** Liza Minnelli James Taylor
Feb. 23: Howard Jones Peter Fonda	**March 3:** Alexander Graham Bell Jackie Joyner-Kersee	**March 13:** Neil Sedaka L. Ron Hubbard
Feb. 24: James Farentino Winslow Homer	**March 4:** Chastity Bono Knute Rockne	**March 14:** Billy Crystal Albert Einstein
Feb. 25: George Harrison Sally Jesse Raphael	**March 5:** Rex Harrison Andy Gibb	**March 15:** George Brent Terence Trent D'Arby
Feb. 26: Jackie Gleason Johnny Cash	**March 6:** Marion Barry Ed McMahon	**March 16:** Jerry Lewis Pat Nixon
Feb. 27: Elizabeth Taylor Ralph Nader	**March 7:** Daniel Travanti Ivan Lendl	**March 17:** Rob Lowe Rudolf Nureyev
Feb. 28: Mario Andretti Gavin MacLeod	**March 8:** Carol Bayer Sager Lynn Redgrave	**March 18:** Vanessa Williams Charley Pride
Feb. 29: Jimmy Dorsey Phyllis Frelich	**March 9:** Bobby Fisher Mickey Gilley	**March 19:** Sirhan Sirhan Bruce Willis
March 1: Robert Conrad David Niven	**March 10:** Bob Green Chuck Norris	**March 20:** William Hurt Mr. (Fred) Rogers

152

January Birthdays

Name	Date	Sign

February Birthdays

Name   Date   Sign

_____

_____

_____

_____

_____

_____

_____

_____

March Birthdays

Name	Date	Sign

April Birthdays

Name	Date	Sign

May Birthdays

Name	Date	Sign

June Birthdays

Name	Date	Sign

July Birthdays

Name	Date	Sign

August Birthdays

Name	Date	Sign

September Birthdays

Name	Date	Sign

October Birthdays

Name	Date	Sign

November Birthdays

Name	Date	Sign

December Birthdays

Name	Date	Sign